MRS. WEBSTER'S GUIDE TO BUSINESS

A dictionary of business terms for today's working women

0   43422 69540   9

Cover illustration by Susanne Starck.
Black & white photo courtesy of Helen Faye Swanell.

Published in Glendale Heights, Illinois
by Great Quotations Publishing Company.

Printed in Hong Kong.

TABLE OF CONTENTS

INTRODUCTION

Having re-defined words from a woman's perspective in **Mrs. Webster's Dictionary**, Mrs. Webster once again turns to her keyboard to write **Mrs. Webster's Guide to Business**. Here, she offers a new perspective for women of the '90's who are diligently trying to juggle careers, home life and, of course, men. She hopes you enjoy reading her humorous takes on every-day life.

"You don't have to be anti-man to be pro-woman."
-Jane Galvin Lewis

BUSINESS 101

"The only place you find success before work is in the dictionary."

--May V. Smith

Resume (re•zoo•ma) n.

A listing of your professional activities
-- with just a little exaggeration.

Business Trip (biz•niz trip) n.

An excursion to an exotic location where all you get to see is the inside of a conference room.

"A man has to be Joe McCarthy to be called ruthless. All a woman has to do is put you on hold."

--Marlo Thomas

Aggressive (a•gres•iv) adj.

When applied to a man, a compliment.
When applied to a woman, a criticism.

College (kol•ij) n.

Where you received your degree in 17th century English literature to prepare for your career in computer programming.

In-Basket (help) n.

An item for testing the weight-bearing capacity of your desk.

Out-Basket (whew) n.

Where you put things to go in someone
else's in basket.

Competitor (kom•pet•i•tor) n.

Someone you would never want to
work for - unless they offer you a
better job than you have now.

"It is plain old hostility that assumes a woman can only get to the top on her back instead of her merit ... if women can sleep their way to the top, how come they aren't there?"

--Ellen Goodman

Sexual Harassment (hay•ba•bee) n.

You'll never know if anyone likes your new outfit, because everyone is afraid to say "you look nice today."

"Numbers really matter. When women reach a critical mass in a field, the cultural barriers naturally begin to slip away."

--Shirley M. Tilghman

Human Resources (per•son•el) n.

The most important resource any business has.

Contacts (kon•taktz) n.

1) What you put in your eyes in the morning. 2) Who you try to market your business to during the day.

Cold Call (kold kal) n.

At work, a telephone solicitation from
someone you have never heard of.
At home, a telephone discussion that
occurs when your boyfriend hasn't
returned your messages for a week.

"There is a clear implication that when ladies are around serious business is suspended. This is not helpful to the careers of business women."

--Judith Martin

Business Lunch (biz•niz lunch) n.

An activity that causes a 15 minute meeting to last 2 hours.

Spillability Factor (oops) n.

A variable that should be considered when ordering food during a business lunch.

"

You may be disappointed if you fail, but you are doomed if you don't try."

--Beverly Sills

Entrepreneur (on•tra•pra•noor)

A woman who has a good idea and the gumption to follow through on it.

Loan Application (mon•ee) n.

" Hello mom...?"

"Being powerful is like being a lady. If you have to tell people you are, you aren't."

--Margaret Thatcher

Experience (eks•peer•e•ens) n.

What your prospective employer wants you to have without paying the salary that accompanies it.

"I think you are just lucky to have something to do that you can really do."

--Katherine Hepburn

Job (job) n.

Something you can't imagine doing for
the rest of your life.

Career (ka•reer) n.

Something you plan on doing for the
rest of your life.

Small Business (smal biz•niz) n.

A company run by a woman who works for 22 hours a day and sleeps for 2 hours a day.

Self Employed (i•am•da•boss) adj.

Working long hours for a demanding boss who never gives you any time off.

"Always be smarter than the people who hire you."

--Lena Horne

Interview (in•ter•vu) n.

An experience not unlike the first date
- you have 5 minutes to impress the
other person, and to decide if you even
want to in the first place.

Bad Timing (no•raiz) n.

Your yearly performance review falls
on the day after the company reports a
drop in revenues.

Good Timing (raiz) n.

Your yearly performance review falls
on the day after your boss receives the
Business Person of the Year Award.

"To love what you do and feel that it matters. How could anything be more fun?"

--Katherine Graham

Work-a-holic (Type A) adj.

A label that sticks to you when your friends call at 10:00 PM and you are still at the office.

Juggling Act (bi•zee) n.

What you perform when your three most important clients all want to talk to you at the same time.

"To be successful, the first thing you do is fall in love with your work."

--Sister Mary Lauretta

Success (sek•ses) n.

When your competition has not only
heard of you, but actually feels
threatened.

Friday Afternoon (TGIF) n.

The most unproductive time in the work-week, and the worst time to schedule a meeting.

Immediately (e•meed•e•at•ly) adv.

When your client wants to receive a product that has been on back order for two months.

Cubicle (ku•bi•kl) n.

Furniture that gets rearranged as soon as you have learned where everyone's desk ~~is~~ was.

THE
DAILY
GRIND

At work, you think of the children you've left at home. At home, you think of the work you've left unfinished."

--Golda Meir

Work (werk) n.

What you say you'll keep doing if you
win the lottery. (Yeah, right.)

"If you want anything said, ask a man. If you want anything done, ask a woman."

--Margaret Thatcher

"The trouble with the rat race is that even if you win, you're still a rat."

--Lily Tomlin

Files (fi•lz) n.

A completely logical system that you can't remember and no one else can understand.

Aspirin (as•prin) n.

With pencils, pens ,paper clips, and antacids, a standard office supply located in your top desk drawer.

"Women should learn to be self-centered, that's not the same as selfish, in the workplace because the workplace is lucky to have them."

--Jane White

Credit (kre•dit) n.

What everyone is willing to take.

Responsibility (re•spons•e•bil•i•tee) n.

What no one is willing to take.

"If you want a place in the sun, you have to put up with a few blisters."

--Abigail Van Buren

Appointment Book (dae•ti•mr) n.

The working woman's survival guide.

Crisis (kri•sis) n.

When your boss's boss's boss's problem becomes your problem.

Monday Morning (blah) n.

A 4-hour period during which the first fifteen minutes completely eliminate the benefits of your weekend.

Coffee pot (kof•ee pot) n.

An attitude adjustment machine.

Desk (desk) n.

The piece of furniture you know is located somewhere under all the papers in your office.

Coffee (kof•ee) n.

The power breakfast of the 90's — the more caffeine and sugar, the better.

Coffee Mug (kof•ee mug) n.

An all-purpose gift for clients, especially with the company logo on it.

"Men and women executives should not kiss each other in public. Even air kissing - the grazing of 2 cheeks in a fake kiss - looks particularly ridiculous in the workplace. And, of course, groping is strictly verboten."

--Letitia Baldridge

ZZZZZ (snore) v.

The sound heard from the back of the
room at every staff meeting.

Last Cup (last•kup) n.

What no one is willing to admit they
took from the coffee pot.

Utopia (u•top•e•a) n.

A land where women are actually paid
what they're worth.

*"Women who aspire to be as good as
men lack ambition."*

--Anonymous

Famous Last Words (sure) n.

"I'll take care of it."

"Deadline!" (ded •lin) n.

"You know about it for 3 weeks,
but ignore it until the night before."

"Take your work seriously, but never yourself."

--Dame Margot Fonteyn

Den Mother (den mu•ther) n.

Who you sometimes feel like when you have a bunch of young employees.

Break Room (brake•rum) n.

The room in any office where you will find the sign "your mother doesn't work here..."

Memo (mem•o) n.

A "short note" that often babbles on
for 14 pages.

Forty Hours (for•tee owers) n.

What you wish your work week was.

Monday (mun•day) n.

What the first day of the week is, regardless of what day it actually falls on.

Window Office (win•do of•is) n.

A desirable location, in part because
you don't have to clean the windows
like you do at home.

Yesterday (yes•ter•dae) n.

When your report was due on your
boss's desk.

Tomorrow (tu•mor•o) n.

When a report that will take you two
weeks to compile is due on your boss's
desk.

"The worst part of success is trying to find someone who is happy for you."

--Bette Midler

Feedback (feed•bak) n.

The noise made by a radio or a boss.

"Work is either fun or drudgery.
It all depends on your attitude.
I like fun."

— Colleen C. Barrett

Zoo (zoo) n.

Where you work, even if there aren't any animals around.

Three-Ring Circus (kra•zee) n.

What your office becomes at the end of the fiscal year.

"Opportunities are usually disguised by hard work, so most people don't recognize them."

--Ann Landers

To-Do List (too•doo list) n.

Where you add items you've already done just so you can cross them off.

Recycling (re•si•kling) n.

A re-working of last year's bad ideas.

Apathy (we•dont•kare) n.

Run (run) v., n.

Verb: How you get from one
appointment to the next.

Noun: The snag that appears in your
nylons while getting from one
appointment to the next.

Eternity (ee•ter•ni•tee) n.

The time interval between 4 p.m. and 5 p.m.

Terminal Hold (ter•min•al hold) n.

Anything longer than 30 seconds.

Crime Wave (krim wav) n.

A perm that frizzes the day of a
meeting with your biggest client.

DRESSED FOR
SUCCESS

"The public does not know what the

proper image of a woman in power is."

--Jolene Unsoeld

Scarf (skarf) n.

An accessory used to cover the baby's spit-up stain on the shoulder of your blouse.

High Heels (waak slow) n.

An accessory to a power suit that announces your presence the minute you step on to an uncarpeted floor.

Elastic (e•las•tik) n.

The best type of waistband to have on
the skirt you are wearing to the office
holiday party.

Fingernails (fin•gr•nalz) n.

Part of the "polished" professional look that makes it impossible to use your keyboard, telephone, etc...

New Clothes (new kloz) n.

What you buy the night before a big
meeting because all your power suits
are at the dry cleaners.

Briefcase (bref•kas) n.

A purse that's been promoted.

Car (kar) n.

Spare closet for your power suit and/or casual clothes for after work.

"Work can make you beautiful. Or at least make people forget you aren't."

--Helen Gurley Brown

Advertising (pra•pa•gan•da) n.

A completely believable promotion that tries to make you think you'll be beautiful and successful if only you buy the right product.

Earrings (eer•engz) n.

A fashion accessory you have to take off every time you place or receive a phone call.

Hemline (hem•lin) n.

What you shouldn't have to shorten to get a raise.

Slip (uh•oh) n.

What you hope doesn't live up to its name during a business meeting.

Patent Pending (shi•nee) n.

You're going to buy shiny black pumps
next weekend.

Scuff marks (skuf•marks) n.

Black smudges that appear on new
shoes the first time you wear them.

Dry Cleaners (dri•klee•nerz) n.

The place that charges $8.00 to clean your white shirt and 99 cents to clean your husband's.

"If you are all wrapped up in yourself, you are overdressed."

--Kate Halvorson

Power Suit (pow•r soot) n.

An authoritative outfit used to enhance clout during meetings.

Tote Bag (tot•bag) n.

Becomes "untote-able" when fully loaded.

Rubber Band (ru•ber•band) n.

An office supply that does just as good a job of holding up your blazer sleeves as the expensive bands you can buy at a department store.

Corporation (kor•po•ra•shen) n.

A term that is rarely confused with cooperation.

CORPORATE SPEAK

"I'm no lady, I'm a member
of Congress, and I'll proceed on that basis."

--Mary Norton

New and Improved (be•ter) adj.

It didn't work the first time.

Marketing (mar•ke•teng) n.

What started out as a flaw is labeled a feature.

"The glass ceiling gets more pliable
when you turn up the heat!"

--Pauline R. Kezer

Policy (pol•i•cee) n.

What you have to follow if you want to
stay employed.

Procedures (pro•ceed•urz) n.

Rules that are put into effect, but no
one seems to follow.

"Over the next few years, the board rooms of America are going to light up with hot flashes."

--Gail Sheehy

Board of Directors
(bored•of•di•rek•torz) n.

A group of people often completely out of touch with the needs of your company and who expect their every whim to be seriously considered.

Forecasting and Planning
(in•da•works)

See Page 251.

CEO (cee•eee•o) n.

Completely Egotistical Oaf - unless the
CEO is you.

"There is no such thing as a non-working mother."

--Hester Mundis

Total Quality Management
(tee•qu•em) n.

The latest catch phrase for "doing things right the first time."

Working Mother (ty•erd) n.

An admirable person who proves that combining the mommy track and a career doesn't result in derailment.

Re-structuring (change) n.

Also known as re-engineering, an activity that usually results in the train getting off track.

Downsizing (lay•off) n.

When your company encourages you to "broaden your employment horizons."

"I never realized until lately that women were supposed to be the inferior sex."

--Katherine Hepburn

100

Good Ole Boys Network (gee•zerz) n.

A TV station that runs archaic
programming.

"If women can run countries, they can run companies."

--Jane White

MBA (em•bee•ay) n.

What women now go to college for
instead of their Mrs. degree.

Labor Saving Device (da•pill) n.

Birth control.

Labor Camp (la•bur•kamp) n.

The annual management weekend
retreat.

Networking (net•wer•king) v.

At home, it's 'gossip.' At the office,
it's 'networking.'

"As it turns out, social scientists have established only one fact about single women's mental health: employment improves it."

--Susan Faludi

Committee (ko•mi•te) n.

A group of three or more people
guaranteed to slow down the
decision-making process by at least two
weeks.

Unemployed (un•em•ploy•d) n.

Archaic. The new, politically correct
term is "vocationally challenged."

Administrative Assistant (real boss) n.

The one person who truly
knows what's going on in
the office.

Capitalization
(ka•pit•ul•i•za•shun) n.

1) Additional funding for your company. 2) Upper case letters on your nameplate.

FINANCIAL

"Whoever said that money can't buy happiness didn't know where to shop."

--Mrs. Webster

Purchase Order (pea•oh) n.

A phone call from your kids asking you to pick up some milk on the way home.

"Death, taxes and childbirth. There's never a convenient time for any of them."

-Margaret Mitchell

Christmas Bonus (too small) n.

Money that doesn't quite cover the additional taxes you have to pay because it puts you in a higher tax bracket.

Stock Tip (stok•tip) n.

Buy low, sell high. If you do buy high,
sell low and use it as a tax write-off.

Raise (raiz) n.

What happened the last time you made bread.

Profit Sharing (pro•fit shar•eng) n.

You know the company is sharing its profits, but you don't know who with.

Cash Flow (kash flo) n.

You watch it flow in, then you watch it flow out.

Small Business Loan (no bucks) n.

What you need because you have no money, but can't get because you have no money.

Bottom Line (ba•tum lin) n.

This refers to your financial status, not
the hemline of your skirt anymore.

Labor Day (lay•ber dae) n.

The day your labors stop covering your taxes and start covering your own expenses.

Comp Time (komp tim) n.

Extra hours you accumulate, but will never have the time to use.

Overtime Pay (o•vur•tim pae) n.

Extra money you accumulate, but will never have the time to spend.

"Do what you love, the creditors will follow."

--Mary Friedman

Financial Statement (pea and ell) n.

I'm broke.

Market Trend (mar•keht• trend) n.

When all the grocery stores have hamburger on sale at the same time.

Market Saturation (mar•ket sat•u•ra•shen) n.

This is only good if you are in the diaper industry.

Non-Profit Organization (no doe) n.

What your new business will be for at least a year.

Stock Option (stok op•shen) n.

At work, the chance to purchase your
company's stock at a discounted rate.
At home, a choice of beef or chicken
for use in your stews and sauces.

Income (in•cuhm) n.

Money that becomes outgo as soon as you get it.

**Financial Planning
(fi•nan•shul plan•eng) n.**

Buying lottery tickets each week.

"Some people are more turned on by money than they are by love. In one respect, they're alike. They're both wonderful as long as they last."

--Abigail Van Buren

Accountant (cpa) n.

Someone who takes your money for counting your money.

Money (kash) n.

Like closet space and chocolate,
something a woman can never have
enough of.

Salary (sal•uh•ree) n.

A 40-hour pay check for a 60-hour
week.

Assets (as•ets) n.

If your male boss says you have a lot
of these, he'd better be talking about
your business skills.

Inventory (in•ven•tor•ee) n.

Stock you want to have on hand, but
don't have room to store.

TECHNOLOGY

"*I don't think necessity is the mother of invention. Invention...arises directly from idleness, posably also from laziness - to save onself trouble.*"

--Agatha Christie

E-mail (ee•male) n.

An electronic form of gossiping (Also see networking).

Computer (kom•pu•ter) n.

The one thing in a woman's life that does what she tells it to.

Hold Music (ee•zee lis•en•eng•) n.

What you are caught singing along with
when the other person picks up the
line.

Conference Call (kon•fur•unz kall) n.

Three or more people who have nothing to say talking to each other at the same time.

Password (xxxx) n.

A "secret code" used to access files on your computer - usually the name of your husband, child or cat.

Crash (krash) v.

What your computer does at 7:00 a.m. as you are typing your report for an 8:00 a.m. meeting.

Vibrator (vi•bray•tor) n.

A pager that causes you to jump at
inopportune moments.

Beeper (bee•pur) n.

A pager that causes 8 adults in an
elevator to suddenly grab their waists.

Information Superhighway
(road trip) n.

The only place your eight-year old can legally drive before you can — and does it better.

Voice Mail (voys •mal) n.

The reason you intentionally make phone calls after hours because you know the conversation will be short.

Lap Top (lap top) n.

What a female employee sometimes has to convince her male boss she is not.

Fax Machine (jus da fax) n.

A device that allows someone in
another state to pile work on your
desk.

Photocopier (zer•ocks) n.

A machine that breaks down when you
need 30 copies for a major presentation
that's in 15 minutes.

Video Conferencing (smile) n.

A technological advance that threatens your ability to conduct early morning phone calls from home — while you are still wearing your PJ's.

User Friendly (uh huh) adj.

What you wish your computer really
was.

Cell Phone (sell fon) n.

Wonderful technology that allows you
to order pizza while stuck in traffic on
the way home.

Virus (vi•russ) n.

What you worry about catching — if
you share your floppy disk with
anyone. (Practice safe software!)

Rationalization (lo•jik) n.

How you justify having time to go to a movie, but not having time to do the paperwork you brought home from the office.

AWAY
FROM THE
OFFICE

"*I think housework is the reason most women go to the office.*"

--Heloise

Birth Control (burth kon•trol) n.

Ten late nights at the office in a row.

Family Planning (u•drive) v.

Deciding who's going to pick up the
kids from day care after work.

Vacation (vay•kay•shun) n.

To him, this means camping. To you,
this means room service.

Golf (golf) n.

A game women should learn to play since that's where most business meetings are held.

"You and I better not stop working because we'd go mad."

--Katherine Hepburn

Day Off (day•ahf) n.

Time during which you worry non-stop about the work piling up at the office instead of relaxing.

Car Pool (kar•pul) n.

On weekdays, what forces you to be on time for work. On weekends, a chance to drive five muddy children home from soccer practice.

Family Leave (nu bay-bee) n.

Maternity leave that's not just for
women any more. Shouldn't this be
called "Family Arrival?"

"*I have yet to hear a man ask for advice on how to combine marriage and a career.*"

--Gloria Steinem

Sick (sik) v.

What your six-year old is when both you and your husband have meetings all day.

Fast Food (McLunch) n.

What you won't let your kids eat, but you have for lunch at least twice a week.

Lunch Hour (lunch owr) n.

When you try to incorporate three days
worth of errands into a fiftynine
minute break.

Hot Water (truh•buhl) n.

What you spend most of the day trying to stay out of, then need to soak in at night to relieve the stress.

Pizza (peet•zuh) n.

What you order for dinner every
Friday night because you are too tired
to cook.

"I hate housework! You make the beds, you do the dishes - and six months later, you have to start all over again."

--Joan Rivers

Day Care (day cair) n.

A paid baby-sitter for your children
usually costing at least as much as you
make.

Rain (rayn) n.

The weather at your annual company
picnic — every year for the last ten
years.

Sick Day (sik day) n.

What you take the first sunny day of
Spring.

Rush Hour (slo mo) n.

Commuting periods during which you slow down to five mph. Shouldn't this be called the stop hour instead?

"When men reach their sixties and retire, they go to pieces. Women go right on cooking."

--Gail Sheehy

Retirement (no werk) n.

What Mrs. Webster can't enjoy because
Mr. Webster is always underfoot.

OTHER TITLES BY GREAT QUOTATIONS PUBLISHING COMPANY

199 Useful Things to Do With A Politician
201 Best Things Ever Said
A Lifetime of Love
A Light Heart Lives Long
A Teacher Is Better Than Two Books
As a Cat Thinketh
Cheatnotes On Life
Chicken Soup
Dear Mr. President
Don't Deliberate...Litigate
Father Knows Best
For Mother - A Bouquet of Sentiment
Golden Years, Golden Words
Happiness Walks On Busy Feet
Heal The World
Hooked on Golf
Hollywords
I'm Not Over The Hill
In Celebration of Women

Interior Design For Idiots
Life's Simple Pleasures
Money For Nothing,Tips For Free
Motivation Magic
Mrs. Webster's Guide To Business
Mrs. Webster's Dictionary
Parenting 101
Reflections
Romantic Rendezvous
The Sports Page
So Many Ways To Say Thank You
The ABC's of Parenting
The Best Of Friends
The Birthday Astrologer
The Little Book of Spiritual Wisdom
The Secret Language of Men
Things You'll Learn, If You Live Long Enoug
Women On Men

GREAT QUOTATIONS PUBLISHING CO.

1967 Quincy Court
Glendale Heights, IL 60139-2045
Phone (708) 582-2800
FAX (708) 582-2813